MW00352639

Vegan in a Van

Healthy, plant-based recipes on the road

Photos, recipes, and writing

By Ashlen K. Wilder

Photographs by Ashlen Wilder

Additional photo credits by Samuel Taylor: bottom cover photo, and photos on page 6 (top), 11 (left, middle), 17, 20 (bottom left, and top right), 28, 41, 96, 102,

Front cover design by Juliana Lopes

Photo of author on back cover by Kirk Hensler + Hale Production Studio

ISBN 978-0-578-80061-5

Acknowledgments

To Owen, my matcha-drinking partner

and to Sam, my co-pilot and fellow
coddiwompler.

I would I also like to acknowledge that we are on native land. I
traveled to many beautiful places in the van, and those beautiful
places were only inhabited by native peoples pre-colonization. Please
recognize, acknowledge, and respect this. Treat the land with
appreciation and respect, and try to leave it better than you found it.

Joe's Valley, Utah

Zion National Park, Utah

Lake Tahoe, California

Contents

Embracing Veganism & Vanlife

Why Vegan?

At the time of writing this book, I have been vegetarian for 10 years and vegan for six of those years. I went vegetarian at the young age of 13, after I started noticing disturbing things about the meat I was eating.

I remember eating chicken nuggets one day while watching seagulls battle over french fries. As I ate the nuggets, I felt as if I was eating the cousin of one of these seagulls. The connection made me sick to my stomach. In my middle school biology class, we watched a short film on pathogens, and the pathogens that could be linked to meat. In the film, a meat processing plant was shown, and I felt my stomach flip when I saw the thousands of pounds of raw beef being processed. Being a bookworm, I walked to a used bookstore in my neighborhood in search of something that would help explain what I was feeling.

Why did my stomach feel queasy when I tried eating meat now? I scoured through books until I found answers. I read about slaughterhouses, factory farming, and how meat was sourced for fast-food restaurants. I later went on the internet to do more research, and there are certain images inside of factory farms that you can't unsee. I was shocked when I found out that sentient beings were treated horrendously for the sake of a meal.

You mean to say that my chicken nuggets, fish n' chips, and cheeseburgers come from abused animals? No thank you. I was appalled that I had spent thirteen years of my life eating something I thought was so normal.

Growing up, I just thought of meat as a part of a normal meal. I loved breakfast sandwiches with sausage, bacon on cheeseburgers, ribs, and chicken nuggets dipped in BBQ sauce. I couldn't unlearn and unsee what I discovered in my research, and now I couldn't look at these foods the same.

Now as an angsty teen, I wanted to do something to rebel. Rejecting the status quo and announcing myself as vegetarian was what I decided to do. Ten years ago, I went to a fast-food place for the very last time. I remember getting a side of fries and a milkshake. Fast food wasn't a big part of my regular diet, but I wanted to do something symbolic to commemorate both becoming vegetarian and swearing off fast food. After that day, I was completely done with meat and fish and haven't turned back.

Committing to vegan

Close to my senior year of high school, I started hearing the word "vegan" float around from some of my conscious friends and trendy restaurants in the area.

Honestly, when I learned what it meant to be vegan, I thought it was ridiculous. I already didn't eat meat or fish, so why would I want to cut more stuff out of my diet?

I was 17, and it was the summer before my senior year of high school. For dinner one night, I ate quiche, and then had an ice cream bar for dessert. I went to my room, and suddenly started feeling cramps in my abdomen about 30 minutes later. I brushed it off and went to sleep.

Around 3 AM, I woke up with terrible stomach pain. I rushed to the bathroom to vomit, and just kept throwing up fluids. There was nothing left in me, but I couldn't stop dry heaving. I had experienced both the stomach flu and food poisoning before, but this felt different.

There was a sharp pain in my abdomen, and I was afraid that I had appendicitis. I went to the hospital, and ended up being there for 6 hours. They checked for appendicitis, but I didn't have it. I got an ultrasound to check for ovarian cancer, and thankfully I did not have that either. After several other tests, it appeared I had a high count of white blood cells, meaning something abnormal was going on.

Anza Borrego, CA

Finally, I had a CAT scan. The scan showed that my intestines were very inflamed; that was why I had elevated white blood cells. An inflamed intestine can be caused by food allergies, sensitivities, stress, and a variety of other factors. I was scared, confused, and lost. My ER discharge papers were vague, and did not include any follow-up instructions. What had upset my intestines so much? What should I avoid eating? Was there something wrong with me on a deeper level? Was I allergic to certain foods? Or was it just food poisoning?

The first thing I ate out of the hospital after the pain went away was vegetable soup. The first movie I watched (5 hours after my release from the hospital) was a documentary on veganism. It discussed the perks of eating a plethora of whole, plant-based foods, and how a diet free of animal products promoted health and longevity. Deep down, I knew I couldn't keep eating dairy, eggs, or processed foods. It was an intuitive, gut feeling.

I went straight to the grocery store and bought a basket full of vegetables. Granted, I didn't know what I was going to do with them, but it was quite the symbolic act. I honestly think I just tried to eat them raw. From that day on, I became vegan. I burned trays of roasted veggies, made very bland tofu, and hated quinoa, but I did it. And I felt 1,000 times better than I had ever felt before. I am proud to say that eight years later I am a much better vegan chef, and now here I am with a cookbook!

I will provide a brief summary of my own reasons for going and staying vegan.

Health Reasons

When I was younger, I had no idea the effect that food had on the body. Food was something you consumed three to four times a day, and you ate what tasted good. Sometimes you ate healthy food when mom cooked black bean burgers for dinner, but most of the time you just ate what was available and offered to you.

Well, after my hospital experience, eating what was available and offered to me was no longer an option. If one of my friends asked if I wanted to cook up some grilled cheese sandwiches for lunch, I had to politely decline. For once in my life, I really had to think about what I was putting in my body, and how it would affect me. Since the hospital had offered no insight into doing food allergy testing or an elimination diet, I had to take it upon myself.

Eliminating dairy was a game changer for me. Without dairy in my diet, my stomach pain, gas, and bloating went away. My skin cleared up from breakouts, and I even had people start commenting on my skin. I had way more energy, and I realized that dairy had probably always been slowing me down. A week after going fully vegan, I went on my regular run which was around 2.5 miles. However, after finishing the 2.5 miles, I had so much energy I didn't want to stop running. I ended up running 5 miles and felt amazing after!

I'm not sure if cutting out eggs made a difference in my body, but it wasn't something I missed from my diet. I found it easier than expected to find new plant-based protein sources, and replaced eggs with nuts, legumes, and seeds.

Additionally, taking wheat out of my diet for several months taught me that that I can only tolerate small amounts of it, and I feel best without it. Most recipes in this book are naturally gluten-free/wheat-free or can be easily modified to be so.

Limiting the amount of sugar in my diet was also incredibly helpful. Today, I notice that if I have too much sugar, I tend to break out, get mood swings, sleep poorly, and experience energy crashes. I suggest alternative sweeteners like coconut sugar and maple syrup in this book because these effect me less than cane sugar.

This is anecdotal evidence of my own experience, but there is a lot of information out there that backs up the health benefits of a vegan or plant-based diet. One book I love , How Not To Die, by MD Michael Greger, discusses in detail how a vegan or plant-based diet can prevent a plethora of maladies.

A plant-based diet can both prevent and reverse coronary heart disease. Plant-based diets are recommended for those at risk for Alzheimer's because this way of eating encourages high consumption of fruits, vegetables, legumes and nuts, and additionally reduces or cuts out meat and dairy. Eating a diet rich in fruits and vegetables while reducing animal products can slow down the growth of certain cancer tumors. Higher consumption of vegetables can reduce the chance of developing depression by up to 62%, and certain compounds found in plant foods can support good mood.(1)

Environmental

As someone who is studying sustainable agriculture in school, I would like to say this section is very important. I am confident you have already heard that veganism is better for the environment. This is actually both true and untrue! Confused? Let me explain.

Concentrated animal feeding operations (CAFOs), animal feeding operations (AFOs), or factory farms that raise cows, chickens, and pigs can be horrible for the environment. This is literally what the USDA defines as an animal feeding operation: "AFOs congregate animals, feed, manure and urine, dead animals, and production operations on a small land area. Feed is brought to the animals rather than the animals grazing or otherwise seeking feed in pastures, fields, or on rangeland. There are approximately 450,000 AFOs in the United States".(2) Yikes. This description is disturbing enough, but these operations can also have negative effects on water, the air/atmosphere, and soil health.

According to an EPA report, CAFOs can pollute streams, rivers, and groundwater from waste runoff that is not well-managed by the operation.(3) Imagine all of the nasty things that are present in a concentrated animal feeding operation; I'm sure you wouldn't want this in your local river or lake. Well, sadly this gross stuff actually does wind up in rivers and lakes.

In the United States, 10% of all greenhouse gases are from agriculture, with a quarter of this percentage coming directly from the methane produced by ruminants like cows. Another 12% of the total agricultural emissions are caused by the release

of methane and nitrous oxide from manure.(4) Globally, 14.5% of all greenhouse gases come from livestock.(5) On top of this, if you have ever driven by a huge animal agriculture operation, you know how bad it stinks. My mind goes directly to the operations I've passed by on the I-5 in California. It's a wretched smell that would make even the strongest of stomachs turn, and a harsh reminder of how I will never consume products from these operations again.

Animals in CAFOs are fed monocropped grains, typically corn. In America, 36% of corn grown is used to feed cattle.(6) Want to know why monocropped and non-organic corn is bad for the environment? Read the first paragraph under "What's the potential issue with veganism?".

Generally, raising cows, pigs, and chickens for meat, milk, and eggs is less energy efficient and more environmentally harmful than just eating plant-based foods. In a study that analyzed the environmental impact of animal and plant-based foods, it was found that meat and other animal-based foods made the largest contribution to the environmental footprints. This study measured the carbon, water, and ecological footprint of different foods, and then found that animal foods had an overall higher footprint than plant foods.(7)

It is important to note that there are ranchers and farmers out there that are striving to incorporate better practices into animal agriculture. Factory farming is not the only way to do animal agriculture. If you are someone who eats animal products, I encourage you to investigate where your animal products are coming from. Look for grass-fed and pasture raised meat and local chicken, eggs, and dairy if you choose to incorporate animal products into your diet.

What's the potential environmental issue with veganism?

Veganism can still be destructive to the environment in a less obvious way. If you are vegan and eat conventionally grown produce, grains, and legumes, then you are contributing your dollars to agricultural practices that are still harmful to the environment. Conventional and industrial agriculture relies on chemicals to kill pests and weeds, which can pollute water, reduce soil nutrients, and reduce biodiversity. Monocropping (growing a large amount of one crop) can cause soil erosion and also reduce biodiversity. (8) Conventional and industrial agriculture also incorporates the practice of tilling the soil intensively, which causes the soil to release carbon dioxide (another greenhouse gas) into the atmosphere. (9)

Additionally, if you are vegan and eat a lot of out-of-season produce or produce not local to your region, this is not environmentally friendly. For example: You live in the U.S., and it's not apple season, but you go ahead and purchase a Pink Lady apple. Check the sticker; chances are the apple is from Peru. That's a long way for an apple to travel, and a lot of fuel used in the process of transporting this precious cargo. Tropical fruits are delicious, but typically they cross an international border or two to get to the U.S. (unless you live in Florida!). Again, that is a lot of fuel for pineapple or papaya to make it into your belly.

It is hard to calculate what is more sustainable; eating a fully vegan diet that includes products from other countries (like mangos, Peruvian apples, and quinoa), or an omnivore diet that includes a high amount of local produce and animal products. Plant-based foods take less energy and resources to produce, but what if it traveled across two countries to get to you? Meat and milk take way more feed and water to produce than a vegetable, but what if it comes from a local farmer? There is no easy answer, but I will say whatever your diet is, I encourage you to buy local as much as you can.

Ethical

I feel like this reason is straightforward. I don't feel the need to take something's life to nourish myself. As a yoga teacher, I practice "ahimsa", which is to do no harm upon others. Many practices in the meat, dairy, and egg industry are absolutely horrendous, and I do not want to contribute my money to these industries. Being vegan is a privilege, and I have the privilege to make decisions about the food I eat. I I have a tight budget, but I do choose to put more money towards food rather than something like new clothes or make-up.

Please Remember...

Being vegan is a privilege. It is a privilege to choose what you eat, and have the liberty to refuse to eat something. Others need to eat what they have in front of them. Others choose to cherish their cultural foods and food they have grown up eating. Others eat a certain way for their health. I ask you as to not shame others about what they eat. When it comes to diet, it is not your job to judge others. Chances are your diet isn't perfect either! If you feel called to educate others, lead by example.

Moving Into A Van

My partner, Sam, and I were living in the small town of Arcata, California. Arcata has an incredibly beautiful landscape of rugged coastline, groves of redwoods, and sprawling farms. You might not have even heard of this small town of 14,000 people (the population goes down to 8,000 in the summer when students leave!). As stunning as it is, the town is pretty isolated.

We were here because I had transferred to Humboldt State University to finish my bachelor's degree in Environmental Science. During my first semester, I was struggling to get full-time work and support myself while attending school full time. I am also a yoga teacher, but the town's studios had no openings. By the end of my first semester, I had $18 in my bank account and I decided I couldn't stay in school or in Arcata for the next semester.

Having to drop out of school and move after I had moved so recently destroyed my self-esteem and self-worth. I had no idea what the next step was at this point. A week before moving, I had a bad fall in a climbing gym and fractured my elbow. To say the least, moving ended up being more miserable.

After all of our stuff was packed, we drove down to my hometown of Santa Barbara; we stayed at a friend's place (Thanks B!) and tried to formulate a plan. I decided that I wanted to give myself a year's break before going back to school. So where would I live? I am from Southern California, so it seemed natural to return to what I considered home. However, it is important to remember that I was quite broke, and Southern California rent is nowhere near being affordable.

We kept circling back to living out of a van. It was a dream of both of ours, and it would be cheaper to live out of than renting in Southern California. It seemed silly, weird, and unconventional, but both of us agreed that we were on the same page.

We both love living minimally, and have always had the dream of building a tiny home. For a summer, I lived in a tiny vintage trailer with my friend. I've also lived in a tent for three months, and one summer I also lived out of my truck, using my tailgate as my kitchen. You could say the small spaces were kind of my jam.

The Van

We were sitting in my favorite brewery in Santa Barbara, skimming through Craigslist for vans. We weren't 100% set on moving into a van yet, but it was slowly starting to turn into our plan A. Then we clicked on a beautiful built-out Dodge Sprinter van, complete with wood floors, cabinets, a king-size bed, a sink, and solar panels. It was everything we wanted, and ready to live out of. Since I still had a fractured elbow at the time, we wanted to instead buy a van that was already built-out, rather than have to do it ourselves.

It had only been listed for a few hours, and we knew it would be sold quickly. After sending an email to the owner, they got back quickly and said that if we were able to drive to San Jose tomorrow, it was ours. Even though it was slightly out of our budget, we knew it was a great deal. First thing the next morning, we were on the road mobbing up to San Jose.

And just like that, it was ours. A big, white Dodge Sprinter that provided a home for two people. How amazing is it that? I would like to note, there was a lot more stress, tears, and struggle involved in this process that I did not want to go into detail on. Figuring out finances and securing remote jobs that we could do on the road was a huge challenge.

The Beauty of Minimalism

Even though I had just downsized a month ago for my last move, another downsizing of my possessions was at hand. I gave away clothes to friends and thrift stores, stored some stuff with my parents, and kept only what was truly necessary. I didn't have much in the first place because I don't like dealing with the responsibility of owning a lot of stuff. Trying to decide what is most important and practical, and what will fit in one vehicle, is not the easiest task.

Luckily, the back of the van had a deep storage compartment so we were able to keep bulky things like climbing stuff and winter clothes back here. It took us a few days to get everything in the right place, and luckily the van already came installed with plenty of cabinets and drawers. I explain what kitchen stuff we decided to bring starting on page 22 . Downsizing to this extent truly makes you realize what possessions are most practical and personally valuable to you.

The Journey

The journey officially started in Santa Barbara, California, and we spent our first night in the van in Ojai, California. We lived in the van for almost a year, and the trip ended in Ann Arbor, Michigan. Here is the rough route we took:

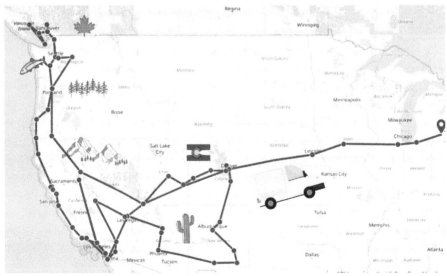

Map created on Travelmap.net & Canva.com

While living in the van, we wanted to visit popular rock climbing spots, go to states we had never visited, explore national and state parks, eat good vegan food, and visit friends and family. I can happily say we did exactly that!

Clockwise starting from the top right: near Bridgeport, CA, Saguaro NP in AZ, Happy Boulders in Bishop, CA, Zion NP in UT

A Tiny Kitchen

The Kitchen Setup

As you would imagine, we had to take a minimalist approach to stocking our kitchen supplies and necessities. As a health coach, recipe developer, and someone who loves cooking, I was not going to resort to eating just cans of beans and soup. No way! I was going to create vegan vanlife gourmet.

As I said before, I have experience living and cooking in small alternative spaces. I like the challenge of organizing a small space, and making that space functional. The idea of creating delicious and healthy meals out of a van did not intimidate me. I can totally understand if you feel intimidated though!

In the "kitchen" of the van, there was a cupboard, a counter, two large drawers a small utensil drawer, and our sink. Under the two large drawers, was the fridge.

The stove - We bought a Coleman Triton Propane 2-Burner Stove. The stove attached to a large propane tank that was on the side of the counter and drawers.

The fridge- The van came with an older model of an Dometic fridge, and included a small freezer section.

The sink- The van had a sink with an electric foot pedal installed. Underneath the sink, we stored 20 gallons of water, and a basic plastic bin caught the waste water.

Cookware & dishware
As campers and rock climbers, we already had some very functional cookware made to be taken outdoors. Here is a rough list of what we brought:
-Stainless steel quart pot with lid
-Small liter stainless steel pot
-Small pot that functions as a pot, bowl, and leftover tupperware
-Small cast iron & large cast iron pan
-3 sizes of bamboo cutting boards
-4 thick glass tupperwares

Continued...

-Sturdy plastic plates
-Sturdy plastic bowls
-A few plastic and titanium sporks
-Metal utensils
-A variety of small and large mason jars
-Our favorite ceramic bowls and mugs
-A few camping mugs
-Measuring cups
-1 teaspoon and 1 tablespoon
-Metal french press
- 2 knives

Specialty Kitchenware

-Handheld frother (battery operated): great for making matcha drinks, hot chocolate, coffee drinks, and dressings.
-Metal percolator: for making strong espresso coffee.
-A handheld spiralizer for spiralizing veggies.
-Ceramic Teapot: yes, this has the potential to break, but I love having tea out of a pot. You could easily not bring a teapot, but just use tea bags or tea strainers instead.

If you will be cooking inside a van, then a smoke detector and carbon monoxide monitor is highly recommended! We also had two fans, which we kept open and running while cooking, and tried to keep the doors open as much as possible.

Some mistakes we made

-Bringing favorite ceramic pieces into the van. Needless to say, most were broken or chipped by the end of the trip.
-Not closing the soap bottle and putting it away. A soapy floor is no fun.
 -Not latching everything down. It is vital to latch down all of the cupboards and drawers before driving off, but this is an easy thing to forget. This is how a lot of the dishware became chipped and broken. This is also how our entire food cupboard spilled onto the floor. The drawers were closed with latches, while the cupboards were shut with climbing cordelette.
-Buying an extra bottle of maple syrup: there was always a crate in the back of the van filled with dry goods, like nuts, cereals and grains. One time, maple syrup was on sale, so we purchased an extra bottle and put it in the crate. It shattered from bumps on a dirt road, and maple syrup coated yoga mats, camping chairs, and wood drawers in the back.
-Putting plastic vitamin bottles above the stove: the heat that rises from the stove started to melt the plastic vitamin bottles. Don't do that!

Kitchen Essentials

My kitchen essentials do not vary much from a normal house kitchen to a van kitchen. These are items I almost use everyday in my cooking! I've divided the essentials into two sections; dry good essentials and basic fresh staples. The dry good essentials are always in the cupboard. These are products that I've used for years, and use everyday. Basic fresh staples are products that make up most of my daily vegan diet, but it is not the same everyday.

Dry Good Essentials
Apple Cider Vinegar
Oats
Rice
Cans of beans
Toasted Sesame Oil
Coconut Oil
Sweetener: Maple syrup, coconut
sugar, or molasses
Coconut aminos or soy aminos
Dried fruit
Seeds + nuts
Nut butter

Basic Fresh Staples
Vegetables
Leafy greens
Fruit
Tofu & tempeh
Probiotic foods
Miso paste
Plant-based milk

Of course, I like to have some specialty things on hand like tea, cookies, dark chocolate, and vegan butter as well!

How I Cook

If I am being totally honest, I hate following recipes. I like cooking with minimal dishes and utensils, so using tablespoons, teaspoons, and measuring cups are a pain for me. It's quite ironic, since I created a cookbook that is essentially just a collection of many recipes.

So why would I do that? I want to show people a fluid way of cooking. I want others to learn how to cook without following a recipe, and feel confident in their creative decisions in the kitchen. Cooking shouldn't be rigid. I understand that baking is rigid with complex rules and chemistry, but cooking doesn't have to be that way. For the sake of you and this book, I have done my best to measure out ingredients in the meals I make the most. I don't think I could call this a cookbook if I didn't have some sort of concrete recipes. There are sections that are more loosely written, like the sections on oatmeal, toast, veggie bowls, and stir fries,

My Cooking Rules:

1. I eyeball most ingredients. I can confidently say that I do not measure out ingredients 98% of the time. My best meals are the ones that don't follow a recipe.

2. Use different colors in your meal! Different colored fruits and veggies have different types of vitamins and minerals.

3. If you're cooking with fresh, local produce, you shouldn't need much for seasonings and sauces. Fresh, local produce has dazzling flavor on its own. The produce shines through on its own, let it have the spotlight!

4. The less dishes, the better. Especially if you live in a van!

How To Use This Cookbook

If you're reading this book, maybe you live in a van, camp a lot, or are traveling on the road. Maybe you live just in a normal house, small apartment, or dorm room. Whatever your living situation is, this book was created to share recipes that are simple, nutritious, and nourishing, yet still minimal and low labor. That being said, do not overcomplicate things. You don't need to plate your food to make it look fancy, or have nice dishes to serve food upon.

If you don't have an ingredient, that's OKAY! Don't feel the need to make a trip to the store to get one or two things. Instead, ask yourself, "How can I substitute this ingredient?".

You don't need to follow the recipes. I loosely follow my own recipes. Think of the recipes as guidelines for you to interpret on your own.

"Salt and pepper to taste" is a phrase you'll commonly see throughout the book. I want you to taste your food as you cook it! Continue to check in on it through the cooking process. Learn how to salt and pepper your food to your liking. Try doing this with spices as well. It's always better to start with less, and then slowly add more.

If you don't like an ingredient in a recipe, replace it with something you love. You're not going to ruin a recipe if you replace spinach with arugula, or black beans with kidney beans. If you eyeball how many carrots should be in the stirfry, it will be fine, I promise!

Find multiple, creative uses for every kitchen utensil you have.

-Try using a colander for both straining pasta AND steaming vegetables + greens.

.-Glass tupperware can be used as extra bowls and plates.

-Sporks save space!

Keep everything clean and tidy

-Remember that small spaces are quick and easy to clean, but also get dirty and unorganized quickly.

-Cooking in a small space can already be challenging enough, but if that space is dirty it will be even more difficult.

Keep a crate of dry goods in the back

-You never know when you might find yourself in a food desert! The only options you might have for hours is gas station food.

-Before driving a long stretch on the road, stock up at an affordable grocery store.

-Dry goods to keep on hand: dried fruit, freeze dried fruit, nuts, sun-dried tomatoes, ramen cups, noodles, bars, cereal, granola, box of cookies and soup cans.

Have a strategy for buying ingredients and making meals

-Since you will have a very small fridge and even smaller pantry of food, you need to be efficient and smart with each ingredient you buy.

-Keep essentials stocked.

-For specific ingredients, such as BBQ sauce, try to make several different recipes with it. You could do the BBQ Salad one night, and then use the sauce to top an Everchanging Bowl another night. Use the BBQ sauce up before you buy another specific ingredient, like pesto.

Water reduction

-If you are living in a van or camping, you certainly will have less water to work with than you would have in a house.

-Be mindful of how much water you use to boil water for pasta and wash produce with. The van had a foot pedal connected to the sink, which helped limit water usage.

-If you are running low on water, you can buy pre-washed greens, and even pre-washed and pre-chopped vegetables. Many stores even carry pre-cooked rice, which just needs to be heated up on a stove.

Breakfast

Pumpkin Chia Seed Pudding

Since we were in the van during Thanksgiving and Halloween, I sadly could not bake anything pumpkin-y. But of course, I still had a craving for pumpkin so this was my solution!

Serves 1

Ingredients:

¼ cup pumpkin puree

⅛ cup chia seed

1-2 teaspoons maple syrup (depending how sweet you want it)

½ teaspoon cinnamon

½ cup plant-based milk

Optional (I highly recommend):

1 tablespoon raisins & walnuts

Pumpkin chia seed pudding layered with pear & pomegranate seeds.

Mix together pumpkin puree, plant-based milk, maple syrup, and cinnamon in a bowl. Add chia seeds. Mix thoroughly. Set aside for 10-30 mins to allow chia seeds to gel up. You can also make this the night before, and this will make the chia seed pudding much thicker! Additionally, you can heat up the milk before mixing it in; this will cause the chia seed pudding to firm up quicker.

Banana Bread Chia Seed Pudding

Serves 1

Ingredients:

½ banana

⅛ cup chia seed

½ teaspoon cinnamon

½ cup plant-based milk

1 tablespoon raisins & walnuts

Mash banana. Mix in cinnamon, raisins, walnuts, and milk. Add chia seeds in last, then mix well. Make the night before, or let mixture thicken in fridge for 10-30 minutes.

Carrot Cake Chia Seed Pudding

Serves 1

Ingredients:

⅛ cup chia seed

1-2 teaspoons of maple syrup

¼ carrot, thinly julienned or spiralized

⅛ cup chopped apple

½ teaspoon of cinnamon

½ cup plant-based milk

1 tablespoon raisins & walnuts

Optional: a splash of orange or lemon juice

Mix together raisins, walnuts, maple syrup, carrot, apple, orange or lemon juice, and milk. Add chia seeds in last, then mix well. Make the night before, or let mixture thicken in fridge for 10-30 minutes.

Magic Cereal Bowl

Cereal can be boring, nutrient-void, and taste a little cardboard-ish. At the same time, cereal can also be cheap, quick, and van-friendly. The Magic Cereal Bowl is my best attempt at making cereal something special! This is a very versatile recipe and as you'll see below there is flexibility with a lot of the ingredients.

Serves 1

Ingredients :

½ cup of granola

½ of Nature's Path Heritage flakes or fruit sweetened corn flakes

1 tablespoon of raisins

1 tablespoon of shredded coconut

1 tablespoon of pumpkin or sunflower seeds

1-2 tablespoon of hemp protein powder

½ tablespoon of nut butter

Top with fruit of choice

1 cup of vanilla hemp milk or any non-dairy milk

It's cereal, don't overthink it.

Plantain Breakfast Plate

Shoutout to my friends from Central America for sharing with me the magic of pan- fried plantain! Plantain is a tasty, sweet starch that can be made savory or sweet.

Serves 1

Ingredients

1 ripe plantain (should be very spotty)

½ cup kale, tightly packed

½ avocado

3 slices tempeh bacon

Thick slices of tomato or a side of salsa

Coconut or soy aminos

Oil of choice for cooking

If you have a larger cast iron or pan, you can make the plantains, kale and bacon all in the same pan.

Peel plantain. Slice into 1/2" rounds. Chop kale.

Turn the stove to medium heat. Drizzle pan with oil. Place plantain slices in pan. Sprinkle with salt. Lay tempeh bacon in pan. Let plantain and tempeh sauté for about 4 minutes on one side, and then flip. After flipping,, add kale to pan. Drizzle kale with a few splashes of coconut or soy aminos. Cook plantain, tempeh, and kale for 4 more minutes. Serve with avocado or tomato/salsa.

Make it Sweet

Sprinkle coconut sugar, cinnamon, & salt on plantain while cooking!

Hemp Protein Pancakes

These are not your traditional fluffy pancakes. The pancakes are rich, dense, and filled with protein-packed ingredients. If you use chocolate hemp protein powder, it almost tastes like dessert for breakfast!

Serves 1, about 2-3 pancakes

Ingredients

1 ripe banana

¼ cup chocolate or vanilla hemp protein powder

¼ cup oats

1 teaspoon of chia seed

Coconut oil for cooking

Smash banana in bowl until all chunks are gone. Mix in hemp protein, oats, and chia seeds.

Heat up pan or cast iron to medium heat. Scoop enough coconut oil into pan so there is a layer covering the entire pan. Divide the "batter" into 2-3 pancakes on the pan.

Try to press the pancakes into a flat disc. I recommend cooking the pancakes on a low heat because the banana can stick to pan at high temperatures. I also cover the pancakes with a lid so the pancakes cook evenly. These pancakes take longer to cook than your average. I would recommend 5 minutes of cook time on each side.

Serve with maple syrup, coconut oil, vegan butter, or a nut butter!

Buckwheat Pancakes

Serves 2

Ingredients

1 cup buckwheat flour

1 teaspoon apple cider vinegar

¼ teaspoon baking soda

½ cup plant-based milk

1 cup water

2 pinches of salt

Vegan butter for cooking and topping

Measure out flour into a bowl. Add salt. Slowly mix in water, and stir. Now turn on pan to medium-high heat. Once flour and water are incorporated well, sprinkle both baking soda and apple cider vinegar over batter. Stir batter gently to incorporate.

Dollop vegan butter onto hot pan, and spread around. Pour batter into desired pancake sizes in the pan. Flip when air bubbles start to form.

Serve with more butter, fruit, syrup and cinnamon.

Breakfast Burrito

If you find yourself in the town of Bishop or Mammoth Lakes, California, you're in luck. These climbing destinations are 40 minutes away from each other and both have coffee shops that serve vegan breakfast burritos. Thank you Black Sheep Coffee Roasters and Stellar Brew; there is nothing more satisfying than eating one of your vegan breakfast burritos on a brisk Eastern Sierra morning. The days after leaving the Eastern Sierras, I always have a craving for a warm bundle of burrito heaven, so this is how this recipe came about.

Serves 2

Ingredients

2 tortillas

½ package of tempeh or tofu

½ sweet potato

½ bell pepper

½ cup kale

½ cup onion

1 avocado

Salt & pepper to taste

Generous sprinkle of smoked paprika, garlic powder, and nutritional yeast

1 tablespoon of vegan butter

Optional: if you have any leftover grains or beans, you can throw it in the mix!

Extras: Vegan cheese? Cilantro? Vegan sour cream? Hot sauce? Salsa? Do it. Add it all if you happen to happen to have it!

Chop all veggies. Melt vegan butter in a pan. Sauté onion and sweet potato first. When onions become translucent, add bell pepper. Crumble in ½ package of tempeh or tofu into the pan. Add all seasonings, plus salt and pepper to taste. Add kale. Sauté until tempeh or tofu becomes golden brown.

Take veggies off the heat. Warm the tortillas over heat, and lay flat on a plate. Spoon on veggie mix onto tortillas. Add avocado, and any toppings you have on hand. Roll up (good luck with this step) and eat!

Oatmeal

As a kid, I thought oats were the most boring breakfast.

As an adult, I have cracked the code for exciting oats, and now eat oats most mornings. I make my oats bright green with matcha powder, or create a decadent breakfast with the addition of cacao. The options for oats are endless, and I am constantly experimenting. In this section, I share my basic oatmeal formula, overnight oats technique, and different oatmeal flavor variations.

Quick and easy

The way I make oats in the van is a method that uses less dishes. I measure out my oats into my bowl, and then add all the extras (coconut oil, nuts, dried fruit, etc.) on top. I boil water on the stove, normally about a ½ cup, and then pour the boiling water on top of my bowl of oats. I cover my bowl with either a cutting board or a plate, and let the oats cook this way for about 5 minutes.

Quick oats or quick rolled oats work best for this cooking process. If you are using a thicker type of oats, like old fashioned oats, these would be better cooked on a stove top. This quick-cook method works best in the van, as opposed to cooking the oats directly on the stovetop. In the van, it can be a pain to wash a pot that is covered in sticky oats. Using the single bowl method reduces dishes and time spent in the kitchen.

Overnight oats

Another easy, efficient way to make oats! I use the same recipes for overnight oats, but with a few changes. Sometimes I will mash ½ banana into the oats, and this works as a natural sweetener. I normally don't add coconut oil to overnight oats because the oil can harden in chunks when put in the fridge. Additionally, I almost always add chia seeds and use a non-dairy milk as the liquid base for my oats.

To make overnight oats, you can follow the basic oats recipe below. Then you can add any variation that is listed on the next page.

The only real difference is instead of adding hot water to the mixture, I put the mixture in a mason jar and add about ½ cup-¾ cup of cold plant-based milk. I make this the night before, store it in the fridge overnight, and it is ready to eat in the A.M. This is ideal for mornings where we go climbing and get an alpine start.

Basic Oatmeal Formula

Directions on page to the left.

- ½ cup of oats
- 1 tablespoon of dried fruit (raisins, currants, dates, blueberries, cranberries..)
- 1 tablespoon nuts (walnuts, pecans, almonds, cashews...)
- Sweetener to taste (coconut sugar, maple syrup, mashed banana)
- 1 tablespoon of seeds (chia, hemp, flax, pumpkin, sunflower...)
- Spoonful of healthy fat (coconut oil, vegan butter, sesame oil, coconut cream, nut butter)
- Pinch of salt

After cooking oats, add fresh toppings like fruit and yogurt.

Matcha oatmeal with sunflower seeds, mulberries, and apple slices

Oatmeal with turmeric powder, hemp seeds, and sunflower seed butter drizzle

Oatmeal with cacao, goji berries, mulberries, chia seeds & peanut butter with a side of yerba mate.

Protein - flavored hemp protein + nut butter drizzle

Classic - raisins, vegan butter, salt, maple syrup or coconut sugar

Chai spice - cook oats in chai tea, or mix in chai spice

Oatmeal Variations

Berry vanilla - fresh or frozen berry variety + vanilla extract + plant-based milk

Turmeric mango - turmeric powder + chopped dried mango or fresh chunks

Matcha mint - matcha powder + peppermint extract

Chocolate mint - cacao + peppermint extract + cacao nibs

Creamy vanilla - vanilla extract + coconut yogurt + salt + toasted coconut chips + chopped dates

-A large bowl of fresh fruit. I love getting local fruit and eating a bowl of these colorful gems for breakfast. This is a very refreshing and hydrating breakfast that is great for the summertime.

-Try different types of toast on page 46 or 52.

-Miso soup! It sounds weird, but it is truly an incredible way to wake up your digestive tract. Page 64.

-Get a smoothie or acai bowl from a local café.

-Treat yourself! Find a vegan bakery or a coffee shop that carries vegan options.

Light
Eats

Sweet Potato Toast

Serves 1-2

Ingredients

1 medium sweet potato

Topping Ideas: Avocado, radish, olive, hummus, garlic spread, shredded carrot, pesto, olive oil, sliced cherry tomato, coconut oil, nut butter, apple slices, cinnamon, maple syrup, strawberries, blueberries, tahini, chocolate spread, coconut yogurt, vegan cream cheese, nuts, seeds. Whatever you can dream of!

Slice sweet potato in half. Starting from the middle, start to thinly slice about 1/4" slices. Try to make a clean cut to the best of your ability. You can slice 1/2 of the potato like this and save the other half for later, or slice the whole thing up if serving 2 people or if you want leftovers.

Grab a pot or pan with a lid. Fill a very thin layer of water in the pot of pan, just enough to cover the bottom. Place your sweet potato toasts into the pot or pan. Cover with a lid, and then bring water to simmer on medium heat.

By keeping the lid on, you will steam the toast. Check on toast after 5 minutes. The toast slices should all be easy to pierce a knife or fork through. If they are still firm, steam for another few minutes. If the water has evaporated, add another very thin layer. When soft, remove from pan and add toppings.

Lettuce Love Boats

Serves 1

Ingredients

3-4 romaine lettuce leaves

½ of an avocado

1 tablespoon of sauerkraut

½ of an apple

1 tablespoon of walnuts

½ cup steamed sweet potato

Chop sweet potato into small cubes or french fry shape. Place pan on medium heat, and add a very shallow layer of water into the pan, just enough to cover the bottom. Add sweet potato, cover with lid. Steam for 5-8 minutes until soft. Drain water, let sweet potato cool.

Assemble lettuce boats. Slice avocado and apple, and place in the center of lettuce leaves. Add cooled sweet potato on top. Sprinkle walnuts and sauerkraut on top. Add any other desired toppings!

Spring Rolls

Serves 2

Ingredients

6-8 rice paper sheets

Fillings:

Tofu, cucumber, bell peppers, apple slices, cilantro, mint, green onion, sprouts, shredded carrot, lettuce, mango, bean sprouts, rice, rice noodles

Wash, chop, and slice desired fillings. Pour a very thin layer of water onto a plate. Lay one rice paper sheet on the plate with water. Let it soak and soften for about 1 minute.

When rice paper becomes soft, transfer carefully to another plate, and add desired fillings on one side of the sheet. Fold ends in, and then roll. Continue this process until desired amount is made.

Dipping sauce: Spring rolls can be dipped into soy sauce, soy aminos, or coconut aminos. A peanut butter dipping sauce can be made by combining peanut butter, coconut aminos (or a replacement), garlic powder, and a bit of water.

Vegan Cheese Board

Yes, this can get expensive quick, but it is so fun to do. Vegans want to be fancy too! I've hosted vegan cheese and wine pairing events throughout the country, including while I was living in the van; maybe I've met you at one of my events!

Ingredients

One fancy vegan cheese (try a Miyoko's Creamery mozzarella wheel or Violife Feta)

Spreadable vegan cheese

Sliced vegan cheese

Something pickled: olives, cornichons, red peppers

Savory spread: mustard, red pepper spread, tapenade

Sweet spread: jam, fig spread, apple butter

Crackers: seedy, plain, herb.

Bread: baguette, sliced sourdough, seedy bread, dark bread

Lay out on cutting board or plate. Pour wine and enjoy!

Mustard Maple Greens

These greens are great to serve on the side of a sandwich, wrap or soup. This recipe can be served as a cold salad or a warm side.

Warm
1 ½ cups of kale, collard greens, or chard

The Flatirons in Boulder, CO.

Cold
1 cup spinach, arugula, or mixed salad greens
Optional: currants, sliced strawberries, or seeds to top

Dressing
½ teaspoon of any mustard
½ teaspoon of maple syrup
½ teaspoon of olive or avocado oil

Cold- wash leafy greens and put on a plate or in bowl. Add optional toppings. Make dressing, drizzle on top, and toss.

Warm - Make dressing. Wash leafy greens, chop finely, and add to pan that is at low-medium temperature. Drizzle dressing on top of greens, and toss in pan until greens are cooked (about 3-5 minutes).

It can be easy to go to a trendy cafe or coffee shop and spend anywhere from $10-$14 on avocado toast. It looks so tasty and fancy, but I promise you can make it yourself, even if you are living in a van or camping!

What you need to know about Toast

Toast can change form to be breakfast, lunch, or dinner...even dessert! It is such a versatile food, which makes it perfect for life on the road. Bread is the ultimate vessel upon which delicious toppings enter your mouth.

Not all bread is created equal!

I avoid bread that is non-organic, contain preservatives, and have many ingredients. Through trial and error, I discovered my digestive system has issues processing low quality bread and non-organic wheat products, and I feel best if I lower or cut out wheat products. I maintain a balance by eating mostly gluten-free bread and products and then sometimes treating myself to regular organic bread from a local bakery that is baked fresh daily. This way I know I am not getting nasty additives and preservatives. Traveling on the road is a great way to try new bakeries and find your favorite loaf of bread in the entire country.

When I do buy regular bread, I buy predominantly sourdough bread. This is my preference because sourdough is a fermented food. Sourdough can be easier to digest, and this works best for my body. Also, the taste of sourdough is hard to beat!

Build your toast

1. **Go to a local bakery.** Buy preferably organic bread, and try to buy bread with 5 ingredients or less! Looking for gluten-free? Some bakeries carry this as an option, but most stores carry GF nowadays.

2. **Slice and toast** on a cast iron or any other pan.

3. **Add a fat** when the toast is still hot. You can spread on vegan butter, coconut oil, drizzled olive oil, coconut butter, or maybe a vegan cream cheese spread.

4. **Choose between sweet or savory** from the list of toast combos below. Or don't choose; I frequently combine sweet and savory flavors on my toast.

5. **Extra Toppings** are always a good idea! I almost always add salt and pepper to savory toasts, and a sprinkle of salt on sweet toast is surprisingly delicious. You can get creative and add chopped nuts, fresh herbs, dried berries, and seeds on top.

Sweet

-PB & J topped with sea salt
-Coconut butter +coconut sugar
-(V) cream cheese + jam
-Maple butter (it's a Canadian thing)
-Banana + nut butter + chocolate chips
-Chocolate spread + strawberries
-Coconut yogurt + figs + maple syrup
-(V) cream cheese + walnuts + dates + cinnamon

Savory

-Pesto + Cherry tomato + hemp seeds
-Avo + lemon juice + pomegranate seeds
-Tempeh bacon + vegan mayo + tomato + greens
-(V) cream cheese + cucumber + sprouts + capers
-Hummus + sun dried tomato + olives + (V) feta
-Avo + kimchi + sesame seeds
-Hummus + green onion + cilantro + toasted seeds
-(V) mozzarella + basil + tomato + balsamic + olive oil
-Avo + sautéed mushrooms + hot sauce (featured on previous page)

(V) = vegan

California Citrus Salad

Serves 1

Ingredients

1½ cups salad greens or spinach

¼ cup of quick pickled beets and onion (page 59)

¼ cup of vegan feta, cubed

¼ cup of halved cherry tomato

2 tablespoons of hemp seed

1 tablespoons walnut

½ orange, segmented

Dressing:

1 tablespoon olive oil

1 tablespoon balsamic vinegar

½ teaspoon maple syrup

Salt and pepper to taste ½ teaspoon of stone ground mustard

Place greens in bowl. Cube feta, halve tomatoes, half and cut orange into smaller segments. Sprinkle hemp seeds and walnuts on top. Add pickled beets and onions. Mix all dressing ingredients, and drizzle on top of salad to serve.

Garlic Broccoli

Serves 2

Ingredients

2 cups broccoli

2 teaspoons of garlic powder or a about 3-4 cloves of garlic

1 tablespoon sesame oil

1 tablespoon of nutritional yeast

Salt and pepper to taste

Wash and chop broccoli into small florets. You can also buy a bag of broccoli that's been washed and chopped already to save time and water.

If using fresh garlic cloves, peel off skin and finely mince.

Set aside. Heat sesame oil in a pan on medium. Add garlic and sauté for 3 minutes.

Add broccoli, nutritional yeast, salt, and pepper. Sauté for about 5-7 minutes.

Carrot, Tempeh and Leek Sauté

Exactly what it sounds like! I had this no-frills dish from the North Coast Co-op in Arcata,, CA and it was a very comforting dish that is easy to whip up.

Serves 2

Ingredients
1 cup carrots
1 leek
1 block tempeh
1 tablespoon of oil
Salt & pepper to taste

Chop carrot and leek into coin shape. Cut tempeh block into small cubes. Heat oil in pan on medium heat.

Add leek, tempeh, and carrot into pan once oil is warm. Season with salt and pepper. Sauté until leek starts to become caramelized, carrots soften, and tempeh is a golden brown color (about 7-10 minutes).

Leftovers Salad or Wrap

Even before living in a van, this was my go-to dish for lunch. I would use whatever leftovers I had from dinner the night before, and add it on top of salad greens or in a wrap. You can add leftover pasta, rice, lentils, beans, etc. on top of salad greens, and then freshen it up with raw veggies and a simple dressing. Leftover veggie stir fries or protein scrambles work very well inside a wrap, especially when you add some avocado, sprouts, or a handful of greens.

Some of my favorite wraps: Cassava flour tortillas, sprouted wheat wraps, almond flour tortillas, raw coconut wraps

Spring Green Salad

Serves 1

Ingredients:

¼ cup fresh or frozen greens peas

¼ cup chopped, quartered cucumber

3-4 mint leaves

1 cup kale

Sliced almond (another nut / seed is fine!)

1 tablespoon of hemp seed

Dressing:

1 tablespoon olive oil

1 tablespoon balsamic vinegar

Generous splash of lemon juice

1 teaspoon of maple syrup

Sprinkle of nutritional yeast

Salt and pepper

Chop kale finely into thin shreds. Place in bowl. Mix dressing in separate container,and then drizzle on top of kale. Massage dressing and kale together with hands for 5 minutes.

If peas are frozen, let them defrost or heat in a pan for 1-2 minutes. Add peas to kale. Chop cucumber and mint, and then add to bowl. Lastly, add in hemp seed and sliced almonds. Mix everything together.

This salad pairs nicely with some grain on the bottom, or a side of toast.

Vegan Greek Pasta Salad

Serves 2

Ingredients

¼ cup thinly sliced red onion

¼ cup (V) feta, cubed

¼ cup chopped cucumber

¼ cup halved cherry tomatoes

½ green bell pepper, chopped small

¼ cup halved olives

1-2 tablespoons hemp seed

1 ½ cups brown rice or quinoa fusilli or bowtie pasta

1 tablespoon lemon juice

Olive oil and balsamic

Salt and pepper

Sprigs of basil

Cook pasta according to directions on box or bag. While cooking, chop, slice, halve and cube veggies + cheese.

Strain pasta, and put back in pot. Drizzle with a generous amount of olive oil and balsamic, stir. Add veggies, olives, hemp seeds, lemon juice, and cheese to pot. Salt and pepper to taste. Top with basil.

Quick Pickled Onion & Beet

This seems like it would be more difficult than it is because when you put it on top of a dish, it makes it look so much fancier. The beet dyes the onion bright pink, making this a colorful addition to any savory dish.

Ingredients

1 large beet or 2 small beets

½ red onion

1 cup vinegar

½ tablespoon salt

Materials needed:

1 small mason jar (16 oz) + lid

Peel or slice off beet skins. Chop beet into small cubes. Add into jar. Thinly slice red onion. Add into jar.

Pour vinegar into jar. Eyeball how much room is left in the jar; it should be about 1 cup.

Pour 1 cup of water into a pot, heat water, and dissolve salt. Pour warm water and salt into jar. Let cool and then lid. The quick pickled beet and onions can be used after a few hours. Keep in fridge or cooler.

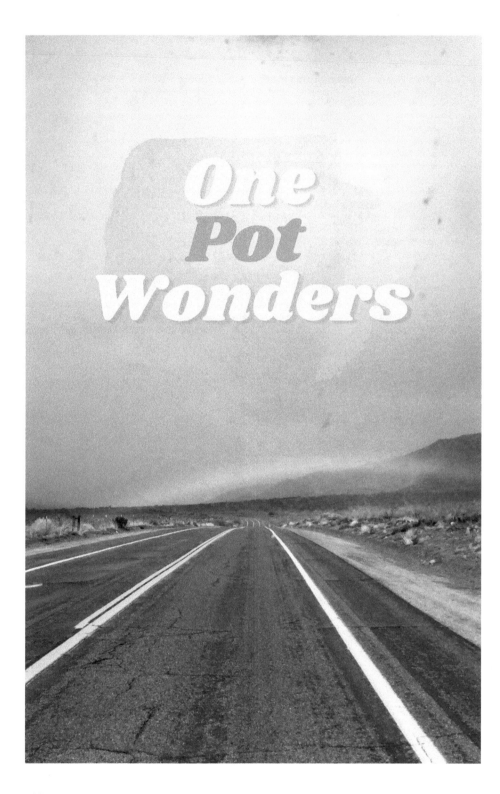

One Pot Wonders

Veggie Pesto Pasta

Serves: 2

Ingredients:

1 ½ cups brown rice, quinoa, or lentil fusilli*

½ cup vegan pesto

1 cup arugula

½ cup shredded or spiralized carrot

½ cup frozen peas

1 tablespoon oil

Any pasta works for this recipe, this is just my personal preference

Bring a pot of water to boil, add a pinch of salt. Add pasta to boiling water, cook for the amount of time listed on the package.

While pasta is cooking, spiralize or shred carrot. If arugula is not washed already, rinse and set aside.

Taste pasta to make sure it is done. Strain pasta. Add pasta back into the pot. Bring to a low heat. Quickly add vegan butter or oil and stir. Add peas in and continue to stir. Add pesto and carrot, stir on low for 3 minutes.

Turn off heat. Add in arugula, gently stir to evenly incorporate. Serve and finish with optional toppings.

Super Lazy Soup Bowl

No recipe needed for this meal! This is a great quick meal if you're exhausted from a long day of adventuring, or just stopping on the road to fix up an easy meal. This recipe elevates a simple can of soup into a more complete meal.

For the super lazy soup bowl you need a can of your favorite vegan soup (I like Amy's Kitchen). Before heating up your can of soup, chop up some veggies to do a quick saute in the same pot you will be using. After veggies have cooked for 3-5 minutes, pour soup on top. Add in any leftovers, like rice, noodles, quinoa, etc. If you have any canned or leftover cooked beans, tofu, or tempeh, this is also a great addition to the pot. Heat soup with added ingredients for 5-7 minutes. Serve when warm with a side of toast or side salad.

Mac n' Cheese

Serves 2

Ingredients:

1 ½ cups of elbow, fusilli, or shell pasta (I like quinoa or rice pasta)

3 slices vegan cheese or ¾ cup shredded vegan cheese

1 teaspoon vegan butter or oil

⅛ cup plant-based milk

¼ cup frozen or fresh peas

¼ cup frozen or fresh corn

½ cup of broccoli

Top with black pepper

Bring a pot of water to boil, add pinch of salt. Add pasta. Check the pasta box to see what the cook time is for the pasta you are using.

While pasta is cooking, cut florets of broccoli into small pieces.

When pasta is done, strain. Keep pasta in the pot. Set back on the stove on low heat. Add milk, butter or oil, broccoli, peas, and corn. Continuously stir the pasta so it does not stick to the pot. Crumble cheese if using slices; add cheese to pot. When cheese is melted and all ingredients are integrated, the meal is done!

Miso Soup

If I had to choose any meal to eat for the rest of my life, it would certainly be miso soup. It's delicious and makes my belly feel happy.

Serves 1

Ingredients:

1 bowlful of water
1 tablespoon miso paste*
1 cup of veggies of choice:
carrot, broccoli, daikon radish,
sweet potato, snap peas...

1-2 leaves of kale or chard (if leaves are large, use just 1)
Optional: Splash of sesame oil & capful of apple cider vinegar (ACV)
For garnish: Green onion and/or cilantro

If I want a more filling miso soup, I will also add tofu, tempeh, chickpeas, leftover rice, or noodles.

*My favorite brand of miso paste is Miso Master. You can find this in the refrigerated section of grocery stores, typically near the tofu & tempeh, There are many different types of miso, like white, red, barley, chickpea, etc. I like to use lighter miso during the summer (white, chickpea) and darker miso during the fall and winter (red, barley).

Chop all veggies and greens. Measure water in bowl you will be eating out of, pour into a pot, and bring to a gentle boil. Add whichever veggies you are using, with the exception of any leafy greens or garnishing herbs. Turn heat down to low, and let veggies simmer in water for 5-7 minutes. Taste veggies after 5 minutes to see if they are soft. Once veggies are cooked, add leafy greens, ACV, and sesame oil.

Miso should never boil because it will destroy the live probiotics in the miso paste. You can now actually turn the burner off before you add the miso. After you add miso, you should see miso "blooms" in the soup. This is a sign that the probiotics are still alive and active. If the water is too hot, you will not have the miso blooms.

To add the miso: Drop the miso paste in the same bowl you will be eating out of. Spoon out about 5 tablespoons of hot water from the pot. Combine this with the miso and stir until there are no more clumps present. This will make it much easier to distribute in the pot of hot water and veggies. Pour the thick miso/water combination into the pot. Give a few stirs to combine. Serve in the same bowl that you used to stir miso in to save dishes. Garnish and done!

Thai Style Curry

After veggie stirfries, curry was probably the most frequently eaten dinner in the van. It's easy, warm, delicious, modifiable and affordable - what better vanlife recipe could you ask for?

Serves 2
Ingredients:
½ jar curry paste
1 can coconut milk
2 cups veggies of choice
1 teaspoon oil
1 can of water

Chop all veggies. Heat oil in pot on medium heat. Add in veggies once oil is warm. Stir for 5 minutes.

After 5 minutes, add curry paste into the veggies. Stir well for 1 minute.

Add coconut milk to pot, and then fill can with water. Add to pot. If you prefer a thicker curry, add less water. Put a lid on pot, and let it simmer for 10-15 minutes.

Eat curry on its own, or serve over rice or noodles!

Congee

Congee is a porridge-like dish that comes from Asian cuisine. In Japan it is called okayu, and in China it is called either congee or jook. This is a great dish to make in the winter and since it has a longer cook time, it will warm up the inside of your van Since this recipe takes longer to cook than others, be mindful of how much fuel you have available for cooking.

Ingredients:

1 cup rice*

4 cups water

½ teaspoon salt

2 cloves of garlic

½ inch of ginger

½ yellow onion

Drizzle of sesame oil

Brown rice is typically used, but white rice can be used if you want a shorter cook time

Toppings: Green onion, cilantro, coconut aminos, sauerkraut, toasted sunflower seeds, hot sauce

Peel garlic and onion, take skin off of ginger. Finely mince garlic and ginger. Thinly slice onion. Heat sesame oil in a pot on medium heat. Add ginger, garlic, and onion to pot.

After cooking for 5 minutes, add water and salt. Add rice. Cover with lid, reduce to a simmer. Cook for 35 minutes to 1 hour & 15 minutes, depending on what rice you used, and how cooked down you want it. If all water is gone after 35 minutes, add more. You can cook it for a shorter amount of time so the rice is more firm and whole, or cook it down until it is a porridge-like consistency.

Once desired consistency is reached, serve with optional toppings.

Vanlife Paella

I thought it was important to put "vanlife" before paella because this is not real paella. This is what you make when you are dreaming about paella, but realize you live in a vehicle and use a camping stove to cook on. Traditional paella uses saffron for the beautiful yellow color, but turmeric is more budget-friendly while still providing a nice flavor and aroma.

Serves 3-4 (Great for leftovers!)

Ingredients

1 cup white rice

2 cloves garlic, minced

¼ of a white onion

½ carrot

½ pasilla pepper (a bell pepper will work)

1 small red radish

⅓ cup green peas, frozen or canned works

¼ cup green olives, halved

Drizzle of oil

3 marinated artichoke hearts

½ can diced tomatoes

½ teaspoon smoked paprika

¼ teaspoon turmeric

1 teaspoon salt

A generous amount of olive oil

3 cups of water

Optional toppings: Salt and pepper to taste, hot sauce, cilantro, lime juice

Mince garlic and slice onion in half moon shapes. Heat oil in a pan on medium heat. Add onions and garlic to pan. Cook for about 5 minutes. While onion and garlic are cooking, chop the carrot, pepper, and radish. Add to pan. Sauté for 5 minutes.

Add in peas. Add 3 cups of water. Add in spices and salt; stir. Add half can of diced tomatoes. Pour rice on top, then mix well. Cut olives, and place on top of rice. Tear apart artichoke hearts, and add on top. Give a final stir, then place lid on pan. Turn heat down to low.

Avoid stirring while rice is cooking. The rice will cook for about 30-40 minutes. About half way through, lift lid to drizzle olive oil on top and add a sprinkle of salt. If the water is evaporated around 20-25 minutes, add ⅓ cup of water. Taste rice around 30 minutes to check if done. If it is still slightly hard, add ⅓ cup more water. Cook until rice is soft.

Serve and add optional toppings.

Shredded Jackfruit Tortilla Soup

Serves 4

Ingredients

½ can young green jackfruit

½ can diced tomatoes

½ bell or pasilla pepper

1 carrot

½ cubed sweet potato

½ of small yellow onion

2 garlic cloves

3 teaspoons taco seasoning

1 tablespoon lime juice

3 cups water

Oil for cooking

Toppings: Tortilla chips, avocado, green onion, extra lime juice, salt

Chop all veggies. Drain jackfruit,
shred with fingers to create a shredded chicken-like texture.

Heat oil in pot on medium heat. Add onion, garlic, jackfruit, and taco seasonings. Stir & sauté for 3 minutes. Add remaining veggies. Add water and canned tomatoes. Taste, and add salt if desired.
Place lid on pot and simmer on low for 15 minutes. Serve with toppings.

Chickpea Scramble

This high protein scramble is an alternative to the traditional tofu scramble. However, you can also replace the chickpeas in this recipe with tofu or tempeh if you'd like.

Serves 1

Ingredients:

½ can chickpeas

2 cloves garlic

⅓ cup sliced onion

⅓ cup cubed sweet potato

½ carrot

2 kale leaves

Sprinkle of smoked paprika

Drizzle of coconut aminos

Generous sprinkle of nutritional yeast

Sesame or coconut oil for cooking

Topping Ideas:

Avocado

Salsa

Leftover pesto

Fresh tomatoes

Green onion

Cilantro

Hot sauce

Coconut aminos

Peel and finely mince garlic. Thinly slice onion. Heat oil in pan on medium heat. Add onion and garlic to pan. Stir.

While onion and garlic cook, chop sweet potato into cubes. Add into pan and stir. Chop carrot into desired shape and add to pan, stir. Wash kale, and cut into thin shreds, set aside.

Open chickpeas and drain. Add chickpeas to pan. Turn heat to low. Add in seasonings and kale. Using a spatula or spoon, mash chickpeas in the pan. After chickpeas are mashed, more oil may be needed if the scramble looks or tastes dry. Taste, and add more seasonings if desired. After chickpeas have been mashed, cook for 3 more minutes. Serve with desired toppings.

Dinner

Veggie Stir Fry 101

Being vegetarian for 10 years and vegan for 6, that probably means I've made hundreds of veggie stir fries. Despite this, I never seem to get sick of them. The veggie stir fry is the foundation of my diet, and it is such a flexible meal.

It doesn't seem possible to run out of variations of this meal. I love a big bowl of veggies for lunch or dinner, and I typically serve a stir fry over a grain so it is more filling. Brown rice, white rice, barley, and farro are my favorites.

When I tell people this is what I mostly eat for dinner, they ask me to send a recipe. Since this recipe is simple but it changes so much, I find it difficult to send a recipe. This is my best attempt at sharing what I eat the most!

The Veggies:
1 cup of veggies per person
(carrots, broccoli, radish, zucchini, squash, parnships, potato, sweet potato, corn, peas, beets...)
½ cup of leafy greens per person
(kale, chard, collard greens, spinach...)

Protein Add-Ins:
Garbanzo beans, black beans, kidney beans, adzuki beans, tofu, tempeh, peas, lentils, chopped nuts

Seasoning, Oil, and Salt:
This is what makes stir-fries truly versatile. You could have the same veggies everyday of the week, but use different spices to make the stir fry totally different. One of the most basic and frequent seasonings I use is garlic, onion, salt, and pepper. Super simple, but perfect.

Seasonings: Garlic, onion, salt & pepper, Cajun seasoning, curry powder, turmeric, apple cider vinegar, taco seasoning, balsamic vinegar, nutritional yeast, hot sauce, Italian seasoning, herbs de Provence
Oil: sesame, coconut, olive, avocado, (v) butter
Salt: Himalayan pink salt, smoked sea salt, soy liquid aminos, coconut aminos, miso, sea salt, ume plum vinegar

Wash and chop veggies and greens. Heat teaspoon of oil in a pan on medium heat. If using onions and garlic, add to pan first. Sauté for 3 minutes. If using potatoes, sweet potatoes, beets, or any other root veggie, add next. Sauté for 3 minutes. Add the rest of the veggies. Add seasoning and salt. Sauté for 3 more minutes.

Add greens if using, optional to add a vinegar or aminos on top of greens. Sauté for 2-5 minutes. Veggie stir fry should be sautéed for 10-15 minutes total. Taste test to check if all veggies are cooked.

The Everchanging Bowl

The ever-changing bowl is the level up from the veggie stir fry; it is served over a base of grain, but with a lot of added extras. The veggie stir fry can be incorporated into a bowl as one of the layers. The ever-changing bowl is my favorite dinners; it has components like leafy greens, colorful produce, plant-based protein, and my favorite toppings, such as avocado and sauerkraut.

This recipe is very reflective of the van lifestyle. The ingredients of this bowl changes as frequently as our location. The vegetables change according to the season and wherever we are located. The components of the bowl change depending on my mood, and that is the beauty of this "recipe".

Kind of like the veggie stir fry, it is challenging to share this as a recipe. Instead, I will attempt to teach you how I build a plant-based bowl. Components of an ever-changing bowl:

Base: a grain; you can use brown rice, quinoa, millet, wild rice, farro, barely, orzo or even cooked pasta if you like.

Veggies: Raw or cooked: refer to the veggie stir fry 101 for inspiration. If using raw veggies, try cutting the veggies in different shapes and styles. I love adding spiralized veggies to my bowls. Go for a rainbow of veggies, and try different veggie combos every time.

Greens: Raw or cooked: kale, chard, arugula, collard greens, frisée, and spinach are some of my favorites.

Protein: tempeh, tofu, chickpeas, beans, nuts, lentils, green peas.

Toppings: Avocado, sprouts, microgreens, seeds, nuts, sauerkraut, kimchi, fresh herbs, dried currants.

Sauce or Dressing:
Balsamic vinegar + olive oil
Tahini + lemon juice + maple syrup + balsamic
Sour cream & dill (page 92)
Coconut aminos & sesame oil
Salsa & vegan sour cream

Arrange all components in a bowl to serve!

Coconut
Dream Noodles

Serves 2

Ingredients:

2 servings thick rice noodles

2 servings veggie stir fry (page 74)
or 1 ½ cups of raw thinly sliced
veggies (carrot , radish, sugar snap
peas, bell pepper...)

Optional: Peanuts for topping

Sauce

½ can coconut milk

2 tablespoons lime juice

5 splashes coconut aminos

½ teaspoon minced ginger

½ teaspoon minced garlic

½ tablespoon coconut sugar

Boil water in pot, and follow directions on packaging to make 2 servings of noodles
While noodles are cooking, chop veggies of choice and keep raw, or make into a quick veggie stir fry.

Strain water from pot, and serve noodles in bowls. Put same pot back on stove, and turn to medium heat. Drizzle a small amount of oil in pot, and add in ginger and garlic. Sauté for 3 minutes. Add in coconut milk, lime juice, coconut aminos, and coconut sugar. Turn heat to low, simmer for 3 more minutes.

Spoon veggies and sauce on top of noodles to serve.

Cauliflower Walnut Chorizo Tacos

Photo featured on page 72

For the cauliflower in this recipe, I actually bought a bag of frozen riced cauliflower. It was very cheap, and saved me the hassle of processing a whole head of cauliflower. You could also buy pre-washed florets to chop up into smaller pieces.

Serves 2

Ingredients:

½ cup diced onion

2 cloves garlic

½ cup cubed potato (any variety)

1 cup riced or finely diced cauliflower

⅓ cup walnut pieces

½ cup chopped veggies of choice (bell pepper, carrot, etc.)

1 teaspoon taco seasoning

4-6 tortillas (corn, cassava, almond, flour...)

Oil for cooking

Splash of lime juice

Coconut aminos or salt to taste

Avocado, cilantro, and salsa for toppings

Dice onion and garlic. Cut potato into cubes. Pull out riced cauliflower if using, or cut up whole cauliflower or florets into small pieces. Cut the veggies of choice into desired shape.

Heat oil on medium heat in pan. Add onion and garlic to pan, sauté for 3 minutes. Add potatoes into pan, turn down heat to medium low and stir. Cook for another 3 minutes, and then add in veggies of choice, cauliflower, and walnuts. Add taco seasoning and lime juice, and more oil if veggies are sticking. Stir well, and then taste.

If more salt is desired, add coconut aminos (the touch if sweetness provides a nice balance) or a sprinkle of salt. Taste. Sauté for another 6-8 minutes.

Heat tortillas, and then spoon in filling. Add desired toppings to serve.

BBQ Salad or Bowl

I secretly love BBQ sauce. I don't eat BBQ products often because I find that a lot of BBQ sauces are either not vegan, or contain a lot of sugar. But sometimes you do what you gotta do to satisfy a craving. I prefer using organic BBQ sauces that are sweetened with molasses or agave, rather than cane sugar or high fructose corn syrup.

Serves 1

Ingredients

½ can of young green jackfruit or ½ cup cubed tofu or tempeh

2 tablespoons of BBQ sauce

½ tomato or 3-4 cherry tomatoes

2 handfuls of salad greens

½ avocado

2 inches sliced cucumber

2 tablespoons corn

A few slices of thinly sliced red onion

Balsamic vinegar + olive oil

Sunflower seeds for topping

Heat pan to low heat, with an optional small splash of oil. If using jackfruit, use hands to shred jackfruit into smaller pieces. If using tofu or tempeh, cut into small cubes. Add to pan. Sauté on low heat for 5 mins.

While jackfruit is cooking, start to arrange salad. Add greens to bottom, drizzle lightly with balsamic vinegar, olive oil, salt & pepper. Slice tomatoes, onions cucumber; add in bowl. Add corn, avocado, and seeds.

Drizzle preferred amount of BBQ sauce on top of jackfruit, tofu, or tempeh. Sauté for 1 more minute. When done, add BBQ jackfruit, tofu, or tempeh on top of salad.

For bowl: instead of using salad greens as a base, use brown rice. Use a small handful of greens on top of brown rice.

Beyond Sausage Plate

I'm normally not a fan of fake meats, and I find that a lot of these products make my stomach hurt because they are so processed. I was please when I tried the Beyond Meat sausages, which are made with pea protein and free of gluten and soy. If you can't get the Beyond Meat brand, feel free to sub out with your vegan sausage of choice.

Serves 2

Ingredients:

2 vegan sausages

Sauerkraut (dill or beet is my favorite!)

2 small red potatoes

2 tablespoons plain vegan yogurt or sour cream

1 teaspoon dried or fresh dill

Salt and pepper

Mustard of choice

Side Salad

2 handfuls arugula

½ chopped apple

1 shredded or spiralized carrot

Splash of lemon juice

Drizzle of olive oil + balsamic

Chop potatoes into cubes. Place in a pot, and then fill pot with water until potatoes are submerged. Sprinkle salt into water. Bring water to a boil, and cook potatoes until soft (around 7 minutes, depending on size of cubes). Once cooked, drain water and let potatoes cool in pot.

Pull out vegan sausages, and cook on medium heat in a pan. If using Beyond Meat sausages, you will not need oil for the pan. While sausages are cooking, assemble the side salad.

Continue to flip sausages so that they cook evenly. Return to the potatoes, and add yogurt or sour cream to the pot. Add in fresh or dried dill, and sprinkle salt and pepper to taste. Mix to incorporate ingredients. Potato salad is done.

Check on sausages. If done, start to plate the meal. Divide sausages, potato salad, and side salad onto two plates. Serve with sauerkraut and mustard to finish.

Ballin' On a Budget Bean & Rice Bowl

Another affordable, easy, and nourishing way to feed yourself on the road. This is a very versitile meal that offers a high amount of protein.

Serves 1

Ingredients

½ cup brown or white rice*

½ cup of beans (black, pinto, refried, kidney...)

Handful of greens (butter lettuce, spinach, arugula...)

Salsa

Avocado

Green onion and/or cilantro

*Can used leftover rice, or if in a hurry, can use a pouch of precooked rice. This can be found in most stores, and just needs to be heated up briefly.

Cook rice according to instructions on bag, or heat up leftover rice or precooked rice. If cooking a new batch of rice, put extra rice away in tupperware and leave serving size out. Add beans to pot that rice is in, mix, and then heat up on low temperature. Add any desired seasonings (salt + pepper, taco seasoning, etc.)

Serve in a bowl, and add the rest of the ingredients as toppings.

Snacks & Desserts

Coconut Whipped Cream

Serves 10

Ingredients:

1 can of coconut cream (canned coconut milk is not thick enough)

1-2 tablespoons maple syrup (depending on your sweetness preference)

Optional: 1 teaspoon of vanilla + lemon juice

Pour can of coconut cream into a medium sized bowl. Add maple syrup, vanilla, and lemon juice (if using). Mix the ingredients together. If the small chunks of coconut cream are difficult to incorporate, use hand frother to beat the clumps or a fork to break clumps.

You can use it right away, or you can place it in the fridge for 1 hour to solidify. Can store in the fridge for about a week. Serve coconut whip cream with: hot chocolate, coffee drinks, pancakes, on top of berries, and any dessert!

Apple Compote

When traveling through the Pacific Northwest during Fall, I made a stop every time I saw an apple tree on the side of the road laden with fruit. Needless to say, I gathered a lot of apples. This is a great recipe if you happen to have too many apples, or have any that are bruised and need to be used up.

Serves 2

Ingredients:

2 apples

1 tablespoon of walnuts

2 teaspoons raisins

¼ cup of water

1 teaspoon of (v) butter or coconut oil

Cinnamon

Sprinkle of salt

Chop apples into cubes. Melt butter or oil on medium heat in pan or pot. Add apples, water, cinnamon, and salt tp pot or pan. Cover with lid, reduce heat to medium low.

Cook for 5 minutes, then add walnuts and raisins, Cook for another 5-10 minutes until desired consistency is reached. Let cool before eating. Goes great with vegan vanilla ice cream or coconut whipped cream.

Almond Butter Chocolate Date Bites

Serves 2

Ingredients:

4 dates

4 squares of dark chocolate, or a few chocolate chips

2 tablespoons nut butter of choice

Cinnamon

Salt

Score a line on each date to open and remove pit. Fill the date cavity with about ½ tablespoon of nut butter. Place a square of chocolate or a few chocolate chips in each date. Top dates with a sprinkle of sea salt and cinnamon.

No-Bake Cookie Dough

Yes, you can eat it raw. You can also make a larger batch of this to have it ready to eat in your fridge or cooler.

Serves 2 (or 1 person who loves dessert)

Ingredients:

½ cup almond flour

1 teaspoon nut butter of choice

1 teaspoon non-dairy milk

1 tablespoon of maple syrup

⅛ cup coconut oil

1 heaping teaspoon of chocolate chips or chunks

Optional: 1 teaspoon of unsweetened shredded coconut

In a small bowl, add almond flour, nut butter, vanilla extract, plant-based milk, and maple syrup. Mix. Melt coconut oil in pot on stovetop. Add to bowl and mix.

Lastly, mix in chocolate chips and shredded coconut (if using). Place cookie dough in the fridge or cooler (or outside in cold weather!) for 15-30 minutes to firm up.

Cast Iron Coconut Pecans

Ingredients

1 cup of raw pecans

1 tablespoon of coconut oil

½ teaspoon of salt

Optional: *you can make a sweet version by sprinkling with sugar and cinnamon.*

Melt coconut oil in cast iron or pan on medium-low. Distribute oil evenly around pan.

When oil is warm and melted, add pecans. Stir the pecans in oil, then sprinkle salt on top. Continue to stir constantly until pecans are toasted a darker brown. If making sweet version, add cinnamon and sugar after 4-5 minutes of stirring. Constant stirring is needed to ensure burning does not occur. Let pecans cool for 10 minutes before eating.

Mini Raspberry Shortcake Cookies

Serves 2

Ingredients

6 Simple Mills toasted pecan cookies*

4 tablespoons coconut whipped cream (page 86)

12 raspberries, fresh or frozen

The Simple Mills cookies are small and crunchy; it's' fine if you decide to use a different brand/cookie.

Flip the cookies flat side up, and lay on a plate. Generously spoon coconut whipped cream on top of the flat side of cookies. Defrost raspberries if using frozen, and place 2 on top of whipped cream to finish.

Pan-Fried Donuts

Sometimes the craving calls and you have to answer. There is no serving size because its up to you how many you want to make. These are featured on page 84.

Ingredients

! can/tube of ready-to-bake vegan flaky biscuits*
Coconut oil
Cinnamon + coconut sugar (or whatever topping you can dream of!)

*Immaculate Baking Co. makes vegan and organic flaky biscuits

Melt coconut oil in a pan on medium heat to distribute a thin layer over the bottom. Pop open can of biscuits and then separate Using a bottle cap or knife, cut out a small circle in the middle of biscuits for donut shape. Place in warm pan, turn down to low, and cover with lid. Donuts should cook for about 15 minutes. Check and flip every few minutes; they are done when golden brown. Coat in cinnamon + sugar while warm.

Hippie Heap

½ apple
½ banana
1 tablespoon nut butter
1 teaspoon maple syrup
1 tablespoon hemp seed
1 tsp cacao nibs
1 tsp raisins
Any other toppings that make you
happy!

Mix maple syrup and nut butter together. Chop apple into cubes and banana into slices. Place in bowl. Drizzle maple nut butter on top, and then add the rest of the toppings.

Sour Cream & Dill Dip

2 tablespoons of fresh or dry dill
½ cup vegan sour cream
1 tablespoon lemon juice
Salt and pepper to taste

Mix everything together. Use to dress salads, drizzle on top of bowls, and to dip vegetables + crackers in. Store in a jar or container in fridge or cooler.

Other Road Trip Friendly Snacks

Raw veggies and and hummus

Hippeas

Tortilla chips and salsa/guacamole

Seedy crackers + vegan cheese spread

(V) yogurt + granola

Apple slices + nut butter

Dried figs + dark chocolate

½ avocado with lemon juice, salt, & pepper

Apple slices + (V) provolone cheese slices

Olives

Curry cashews

Figs topped with coconut yogurt

Sprouted tortilla + vegan butter + cinnamon

Almond flour tortilla with peanut butter and jelly

Trail mix

Freeze dried fruit

Dolmas

Dark chocolate squares

Nori sheets

Cherry tomatoes + salt & pepper

Drinks

Morning Drink

I have this every morning! I'll make this drink first thing when I wake up, and then take sips of it while I'm doing yoga. Most mornings I have the basic version, but I do like to switch it up with other variations.

Serves 1

Ingredients

8 oz warm water

1 capful of apple cider vinegar

Splash of lemon juice

Variations

-sliced ginger

-cayenne

-cinnamon

-elderberry syrup

Warm water on stove and add in desired ingredients and variations.

Kukicha Tea

Even though this isn't a recipe, kukicha tea deserves a space in this book. Popular as a beverage in the macrobiotic diet, kukicha tea is rich in minerals and excellent for digestion. It is made from the roasted stems of green tea. I drank this frequently in the van, as it is excellent for long stretches on the road. It is energizing and revitalizing without any caffeine!

Mint Tea + Apple Juice

I love drinking mint tea at night, so I frequently make extra tea and save some to put it in the fridge overnight. The next day I have cold mint tea, and can use it to make this simply refreshing drink.

Serves 1
Mix together
1 cup of cold mint tea
½ cup apple juice

Mason Jar Iced Tea

This was great to prep in the morning before driving. It takes a few hours to brew, so by the time the day was hot, there would be a cold jar of iced tea in the fridge.

Serves 2
Mix together
¼ cup tea of choice
32 oz room temp water

Measure out tea into 32 oz mason jar. Fill jar up with water, lid, then place in fridge or cooler for 2-5 hours depending on desired strength of tea.

Hot Cacao

You can use regular cocoa, but I prefer the richness and flavor of cacao.

Serves 1
Ingredients
1 cup of oat milk
1 heaping tablespoon cacao
1-2 teaspoons sweetener of choice

Heat milk on stove, be careful not to boil. Add in cacao and sweetener, mix in with hand frother or whisk.

Make it minty

By adding in a peppermint tea bag or 1 drop of peppermint essential oil.

Cold Brew Coffee

No need for all the fancy cold brew coffee equipment! This simple recipe will save you spending $5 on cold brew at a trendy coffee shop.

Needed:

32 oz mason jar

¼ cup ground coffee

Strainer (this is optional)

Enough water to fill the mason jar

Add ground coffee to mason jar. Fill a mason jar to the top with filtered water. If you want to make your cold brew extra smooth and not bitter try using alkaline water.

Put jar in fridge or cooler for 14-24 hours, depending on how strong you want it.

When the brew has reached desired strength, use a strainer over another container or jar to separate the grinds from the brew. If you don't have a strainer, you can actually use the lid of the mason jar to do this. Take the rim off of the circle part of the lid. Place the metal circle over mason jar open, and shift it so there is a very small opening. Pour the cold brew into another container or jar, and try not to let the grinds escape through the opening.

Note: If you've made a very strong cold brew, you can always add some oat milk or coconut creamer.

Yerba Mate

Before yerba mate, I was a coffee drinker during the end of high school and beginning of college. Someone introduced me to yerba mate, and I was infatuated. Yerba mate is a lot less acidic than coffee, and not only is it strongly caffeinated, it is also a mood booster. Coffee can often hurt my stomach due to the acidity, and make me feel anxious and jittery. If you also experience this, I recommend trying out yerba mate or matcha.

Yerba mate comes in individual tea bags or as loose leaf tea in a bag. I typically buy it loose leaf since it is more affordable, and I like to brew my yerba mate more potent. When you heat water to make yerba mate, you want to make sure that you do not boil it, becuase this will negatively affect the taste of it,

Different ways to brew yerba mate:

-French press

-Teapot

-Teabag

-Gourd + Bombilla - This is the traditional way to drink yerba mate. You can see what this looks like on page 42. You can easily buy a gourd and bombilla online, or you could find these items at a tea shop or health food store. Also, if you just buy the bombilla, the straw that works as a filter, you could just stick it in a normal mug to drink the mate. This is pictured on the bottom right.

Variations:

Put in fridge for iced yerba mate

Add apple juice to iced yerba mate

Add mint to hot or iced mate

Add plant milk to make a hot or iced latte

Top photo: Hot springs near Bishop, CA
Bottom Photo: Sedona, AZ

Matcha is trending in the health food world right now, and for good reason. You may have seen this bright green powder before, which is made from grinding young, green tea leaves. So instead of steeping green tea leaves, you are actually ingesting the whole leaf. Matcha is high in L-Theanine, the compound that reduces stress and boosts your mood. It has less caffeine than yerba mate and coffee, but is still energizing.

Because of the color, it is really fun to play with in the kitchen! Try adding it to oats, chia seed pudding, dressings, or making these tasty drinks.

Heads up, not all matcha is equal! Some brands, even more expensive brands I've bought, are low quality. You can tell the quality of matcha by its color. Matcha should not have a yellow or brown hue; high quality matcha should be bright green. High quality matcha tastes vegetal, slightly sweet, silky, with a balance of bitterness. Low quality matcha will lack that complex flavor palate and only taste bitter.

Oat Milk Matcha Latte

My go-to basic matcha latte recipe. It can be made hot, or over ice!

Serves 1
Ingredients
1 teaspoon matcha
1-2 teaspoons of coconut sugar or maple syrup
1 cup of unsweetened oat milk

If making a hot latte, heat oat milk on medium heat. Do not let boil, and take off heat once the milk starts to steam. Pour about 1 inch of milk into mug. Add matcha and sweetener of choice to milk. Use handheld frother to mix. Pour rest of milk into mug.

If making an iced latte, follow exact same steps, except for heating up the milk. After matcha and sweetener have been mixed into the milk, add ice as the last step.

Matcha Variations

Follow the same directions as above for making a hot or iced drink. Add variations in when combining matcha with milk.

Variations
Rose - spritz with rose water
Mint- add peppermint essential oil
Mocha - add 1 teaspoon cacao
Cinnamon Vanilla - splash of vanilla extract + sprinkle of cinnamon

Tropical Sake Lemon Drop

If you can't find coconut flavored water, try another tropical flavor like mango or passionfruit.

Serves 1
Mix Together
4 oz of unfiltered sake
1 tablespoon lemon juice
4oz of coconut flavored sparkling water

La crux

Serves 1
Mix together
1 oz tequila of choice
Flavored sparkling water of choice

Best served over ice.

Pictured: Cherry-berry kombucha, tequila, juice of ½ lemon, and pomegranate seeds in Joshua Tree National Park.

Serves 1

Mix together:

½ of a Kombucha bottle (about 8 oz)

Juice of ½ of a lemon, orange or lime + garnish

1 oz of tequila, mezcal, gin or vodka

optional: add in mint or fruits

White Canadian

Sam is Canadian, and we made this drink while traveling through British Columbia. His grandma made a drink similar to this, so this is a homage to her creation.

Serves 1

Mix together

1 cup of oat milk

1 oz Crown Royal

1 tablespoon maple syrup

Sprinkle of cinnamon

Serve over ice or warm

Squamish, British Columbia

End Notes

Favorite Eateries, Cafés & Breweries Along the Way

California

Mony's Mexican Food (Santa Barbara)
Natural Cafe (Santa Barbara)
Figueroa Mountain Brewery (Santa Barbara)
Farmer & the Cook (Ojai)
Modern Times (San Diego)
OB People's Organic Food Market (San Diego)
The Grain Cafe (Los Angeles)
Natural Sisters Cafe (Joshua Tree)
Chef Tanya's Kitchen (Palm Springs)
Bliss Cafe (San Luis Obispo)
Bagelry (Santa Cruz)
Steep Organic Coffee & Tea (Hopland)
Nourish Cafe (San Francisco)
Phoenix Cafe (Arcata)
Wildflower Cafe (Arcata)
Redwood Curtain (Arcata)
Stellar Brew (Mammoth Lakes)
Black Sheep Coffee Roasters (Bishop)

Arizona

Firecreek Coffee (Flagstaff)

New Mexico

Thai Vegan (Albuquerque)

Colorado

Copeka Coffee (Grand Junction)
Black Project Brewery (Denver)
City O' City (Denver)
Watercourse Foods (Denver)
Wild Women Wine (Denver)

Utah

Moab Kitchen (Moab)
Moab Coffee Roasters (Moab)
Cup of Joes (Orangeville)
Deep Creek Coffee Company (near Zion NP)

Oregon

Sweetpea Baking Company (Portland)
Vtopia (Portland)
Tao of Tea (Portland)
Cascade Brewing (Portland)
Dobra Tea (Ashland)

Washington

Schweinhaus Biergarten (Bellingham)

British Columbia

Green Cuisine (Victoria)
The Green Mustache (Squamish)

References

1. Greger, Michael. *How Not To Die*. London, UK: Pan Books, 2017.

2. "Animal Feeding Operations".Natural Resources Conservation Service. United Stated Department of Agriculture .
https://www.nrcs.usda.gov/wps/portal/nrcs/main/national/plantsanimals/livestoc k/afo/.

3. Hutchins, Stephen R, Mark V. White, and Susan C. Mravik. "Case Studies on the Impact of Concentrated Animal Feeding Operations (CAFOs) on Ground Water Quality ." EPA. Environmental Protection Agency , September 2012.
https://archive.epa.gov/ada/web/pdf/p100f9di.pdf.

4. "Sources of Greenhouse Gas Emissions." EPA. Environmental Protection Agency, September 9, 2020. https://www.epa.gov/ghgemissions/sources-greenhouse-gas-emissions.

5. "By the numbers: GHG emissions by livestock". Food and Agriculture Organization of the United Nations. http://www.fao.org/news/story/en/item/197623/icode/

6 Foley, Jonathan. "It's Time to Rethink America's Corn System," March 5, 2013.
https://www.scientificamerican.com/article/time-to-rethink-corn/.

7. Rosi, A., Mena, P., Pellegrini, N. et al. Environmental impact of omnivorous, ovo-lacto-vegetarian, and vegan diet. Sci Rep 7, 6105 (2017).
https://doi.org/10.1038/s41598-017-06466-8

8. "Organic vs Conventional." Rodale Institute, December 3, 2018.
https://rodaleinstitute.org/why-organic/organic-basics/organic-vs-conventional/.

9."Climate Change." Rodale Institute, September 25, 2020.
https://rodaleinstitute.org/why-organic/issues-and-priorities/climate-change/.

About This Book

As the title of this book suggests, the recipes in this book were created while I lived in a Dodge Sprinter van. Over a total of 11 months, I learned how to create 3 meals a day in a space that totaled around 86 square feet, without sacrificing taste, veganism, or nutrition. I started writing down recipes and taking photos while living in the van, and finished writing the book after moving out of and selling the van. Since many of the photos were taken while living in the van, they are not "professional", and all of the photos of food were taken on an iPhone.

As I finish writing this book, I am actually in the process of buying another smaller van so I can get back to exploring on the road!

Self Publishing

This book was 100% self-published. I, the author Ashlen Wilder, am also the recipe developer, food photographer, film photographer, editor, designer, and publisher. Shoutout to my mom for going over edits with me! Thank you for purchasing this book to support this ambitious endeavor of mine.

Film Photography

If any of the photos have a vintage or retro feel, it's because they are probably film photos. All of the photos of nature in this book are from our journey, and most are shot on either a Yashica or Pentax film camera.

CPSIA information can be obtained
at www.ICGtesting.com
Printed in the USA
JSHW050207080222
22682JS00005B/20